THE
Woodhall Spa
GUIDE

by
Edward Mayor

Photographs and origination by Kathryn Fairs
Additional photography by Neil Storey and George Fairs
Old postcards supplied by Alan Underwood

First Published in Great Britain in 2007 by Silver Rivers Books
14 Iddesleigh Road, Woodhall Spa, Lincolnshire LN10 6SR
Text © Edward Mayor
All rights reserved
Design © TUCANN*design&print*
Distributed by: The Book Fayre • 01526 354501
www.thebookfayre.com

ISBN 978-0-9556730-0-9

Produced by: TUCANN*design&print*, 19 High Street, Heighington, Lincoln LN4 1RG
Tel & Fax: 01522 790009 • www.tucann.co.uk

Acknowledgements

Richard Todd, film star and regular visitor to Woodhall Spa in connection with his role as Guy Gibson in the film 'The Dambusters', sent his best wishes for this project from his home near Grantham. I am very grateful to Mrs Sally Hotchkin for supplying an image of Thomas Hotchkin, the true founder of Woodhall Spa. The Hotchkin family have been central to the Spa's story, and always so generous.

Kathryn Fairs realised the need for this Guide following decades of handsome but brief official guides and pamphlets. She offered me this wonderful opportunity to celebrate the place I have loved since childhood, and opened many doors for me, taking new photographs and sparkling with enthusiasm throughout. She has also organised the Information section. Her husband Reg Fairs helped greatly and advised on local RAF history. Janet Hunt ensured that a procession of local people and visitors were propelled towards me in her Tea Rooms in case they could add anything of interest. Neil Storey kindly supplied additional photographs, as did Jonathan Perks, and Alan Underwood (the Spa's 'Mr Music') enabled us to draw upon his superb collection of old postcards.

Marjorie Sargeant's books about old Woodhall Spa have been invaluable and her personal support much appreciated. David Radford, catalyst of the Cottage Museum, kindly put me in touch with Bob Ritson who is currently researching the Spa's main architect Richard Adolphus Came. The Directors of the Museum and members of the local heritage group have been very helpful and co-operative, as have the librarians of all the local libraries. Once again I am indebted to David Robinson OBE, whose beautiful 'Book of Horncastle and Woodhall Spa' provides a sound basis for further research. East Lindsey District Council kindly allowed the use of their excellent tourist map, while David Start of Heritage Lincolnshire kindly shared the latest thinking on Kirkstead's Abbey and St. Leonard's Church.

Narendra Patel and his staff at the Golf Hotel and Aqua Santé' Spa kindly shared many key documents about his recent restoration of the 'Spa' element to Woodhall, while Ian Macdonald kindly granted permission for a good look around the Manor House, where we received a warm welcome. Richard Latham, the Spa's Director of Golf, clarified many points and was most hospitable. Tonia Oldham of the Oglee Guest House and the Stennetts of Kirkstead's Station House shared a lot of information and were most welcoming. Guy Newton and Hugh Croft, whose memories go back a long way, gave me many insights, some of them unprintable in a Guide Book! Jeremy Walsh of Hoby Hotels kindly supplied a history of the Woodhall Spa Hotel. Mr Bisbey of the Methodist Church was most helpful.

Indirectly, my friends at the Petwood Hotel and the Kinema in the Woods have helped and supported the Guide via the books they kindly commissioned from me some years ago. I greatly value a very happy association with them, and now with a growing number of Woodhall Spa's institutions which have made a big difference to life here, both for the locals and the visitors. The local Parish Council and Rotary Clubs, local Lions groups, organisers of playgroups and many more have improved facilities, involved the community, and forged partnerships. Special thanks go to Wendy Radford, Clerk to the Parish Council.

Finally and as always my thanks go to my partner Jonathan and our famous terrier, Rosie. Their love is unconditional, but you need to have a biscuit handy for Rosie!

Thank you all.
Edward Mayor. Summer 2007.
© Edward Mayor

Contents

The Woodhall Spa Guide
Introduction

The Dambusters Memorial drawn by Edward Mayor

Woodhall Spa is unique. Markedly different from Lincolnshire's other beautiful villages, it seems to be on permanent holiday, and has long been known as an inland resort. John Betjeman and Nikolaus Pevsner remarked on the comfortable affluence of the houses and hotels which looked as though they belonged more to Bournemouth or Droitwich. The four grand avenues leading into this Main Village are broad, floral and tree lined, and substantial remnants of a planned garden village which grew up at the side of the Spa in the 1890s are in evidence wherever you look.

Ralph Townley in his 'The Brides of Enderby' says 'in 1890 a Bavarian came and planned, and eventually built with local capital, a miniature Baden Baden'. Richard Adolphus Came, whose practice was in London's Mecklenburg Square, was certainly not Bavarian, but many visitors to Woodhall Spa did indeed come from Baden Baden, Bad Kreuznach and the like, because Woodhall's waters were far richer in bromine and iodine than their own.

The Original Spa Bath House, in the late 1830's.

The original Spa Bath House in the late 1830s

Woodhall Spa has other unique facilities including the famous Kinema in the Woods and a Golf Course so fine that it has continually ranked in the top 50 courses of the entire world. It is also reckoned the finest inland course in Britain. And Woodhall Spa is now the headquarters of the English Golf Union. Meanwhile, its Spa treatments, dormant since the 1980s, are now restored at the Golf Hotel's Aqua Santé Spa, and a dramatic expansion of facilities is proposed.

The Spa retains its charm despite the fact that so many features have vanished. The guide devotes a chapter to these, which include the railway and its station, which to quote Ralph Townley again was "the toy-sized railway station with its elaborate fretwork and moss lined hanging baskets trailing fuchsia almost to the platform". Onto that platform stepped royalty, aristocracy and hosts of people in need of a therapeutic break walking in the pine woods, listening to several orchestras, golfing, riding, or in cold weather simply sheltering in the Winter Gardens.

Postcards from Alan Underwood's superb collection enable us to see the opulence of the Spa in its late Victorian and Edwardian heyday. A map will lead to the numbered entries in Part 4 "Woodhall Today", and a series of suggested walks will bring you into contact with Woodhall Spa Old and New. For those interested in wartime Aviation history, tours of local airfields and museums are included. A number of well received publications have set down a substantial recorded history of the Spa in recent years, and these are listed at the end. It is hoped that this first comprehensive guide will enable the visitor to engage with the magic, majesty and peace of one of the most beautiful places in Britain.

Edward Mayor 2007

Note[1] : *Came was certainly educated in Germany. Unfortunately, Ralph Townley died in 1999 and although 'Came' and 'Adolphus' are not English names, RA Came's birth certificate states he was born in Islington and that his father was an office messenger with the East India Company. See separate entry on Came.*

Part One
Ancient History

Although Woodhall Spa is an invention of the 19th Century, The Domesday Book of 1086 mentions 'Woodhall' in the following entry:

> 'In the jurisdiction of Queen Edith's Manor, Langton near Horncastle, and Torp in Woodhall 3 carucates of land. There are 13 sokemen and 24 villans have 4 ploughs, and 1 mill rendering 9s and 120 acres of meadows and 250 acres of woodland pasture.'

Kirkstead was not mentioned, probably because its great Cistercian Abbey, founded by Hugo de Brito in 1139, had yet to be built. A Cistercian Priory at Stixwould was founded at the same time.

There had been a moated manor house in Woodhall in the 14th Century together with a few cottages and farms, and the church of St. Margaret, demolished in 1973, had been a 14th century building. But the land to the south of Woodhall was sandy heathland with bogs, with a moor rising to the south, and at its highest point, the Lord Treasurer of England, Ralph Cromwell, 'builded a pretty turret, called the Tower on the Moore', it is thought as a hunting lodge. Perhaps this was the first building in the area that became Woodhall Spa, and it must have followed closely upon the building of Cromwell's home, Tattershall Castle, which he began in 1434 after becoming Treasurer. Today, only the staircase corner of the red

The 'Tower on the Moore', built by Ralph Cromwell in the mid 15th Century
Photograph by Jonathan Perks

brick tower on the moor remains, visible from the Hotchkin Golf Course and the main Horncastle Road. It has become the symbol of Woodhall Spa.

In the 17th century, Woodhall was called Buckland, but it would become Old Woodhall after a series of events which resulted in the founding of Woodhall Spa in the 1830s. Meanwhile, in the 18th century, a Manor House was built at the southern tip of Bracken Wood, not far from the Tower on the Moor, while Kirkstead had developed, with its 17th century Hall (built from stones from the Abbey). On the 1824 Ordnance Survey map, the Woodhall Spa area was a mixture of woodland and moorland, with today's main roads already established as lanes.

Enter John Parkinson Junior

Sir Joseph Banks of Revesby, the great botanist, approved a scheme for draining several local fens in 1800. The resulting changes in the landscape signalled an ideal time to invest in land. Banks' land agent and steward of his Lincolnshire Estates was one John Parkinson, who introduced his son to the network of local landowners. John Parkinson Junior was eager to capitalise on all he had learned, and desired to 'sink a coal mine, plant a forest, and build a city.' He bought, between 1796 and 1821, a lot of local land and planted three woods (Kirkby Wood, Kirkby Low Wood, and Roughton). Sadly, the trees took years to grow, and bankruptcy dogged Parkinson, resulting in the sale of Kirkby Wood to his solicitor and agent, William Ostler, hence the 'Ostler's Plantation' on today's maps. Parkinson also built houses, but hardly a city, at New Bolingbroke. He hired a mining expert and according to some authorities, mining commenced at 'Coal Pit Wood' in 1811 and actually yielded small amounts of coal until the miners grew so desperate that they took coal down the mine in their pockets in order to bring it up! 1811 is also the date given by the Woodland Trust for the planting of a wood to provide the pit-props. The mine was abandoned in 1823-4, but it filled with water from underground springs – a momentous event.

Enter Thomas Hotchkin, Lord of the Manor and true founder of Woodhall Spa

Thomas Hotchkin had tasted the water from the mine and eventually found it beneficial for his gout. Others also found it helped their rheumatism and arthritis. So, having bought the land around the coal pit from Parkinson, Hotchkin erected a windlass over the shaft and drew water into a brick-lined bath. In the same year, 1838, he also built a Pump Room and Bath House, then, in about 1839, the Victoria Hotel. Parkinson died in 1858, aged 86, just as the Spa was coming into its own.

Thomas Hotchkin, from an original miniature painting in the collection of Mrs Sally Hotchkin

Stafford Hotchkin sells the Spa.

Stafford, Thomas's son, sought to involve wealthy entrepreneurs in the Spa, and refurbished the Victoria Hotel in 1884, selling 75 acres including the hotel and Bath House, to a syndicate in 1887. The Rev. J. O. Stephens of Blankney masterminded the syndicate, which included three Members of Parliament: Edward Stanhope, Sir Richard Webster, and the Rt. Hon. H. Chaplin. They made great improvements and invited an architect from London, Richard Adolphus Came, to plan a model garden village with wide, tree-lined boulevards, half-timbered rows of shops, several large guesthouses, and a further hotel, the Royal Hotel, in which Came lived before settling in Woodhall Spa for the rest of his life.

Golf, Cricket and the Outdoor Life

A trophy of fruits in the Jubilee Park, completely hidden by foliage in the summer

The Hotchkin family developed golf in the Spa (see entry on Golf Course) while the newly married Weigalls, at the enlarged Petwood house, developed cricket grounds and many other outdoor activities in the extensive grounds bordering the Stixwould Road. They effectively left the village in 1934, re-visiting annually and eventually presenting Jubilee Park to the people of Woodhall Spa in 1947. Their efforts saved the Spa Baths on several occasions and their generosity to many families and local organisations has become a local legend. (See entries on Petwood House and Jubilee Park).

The rest of Woodhall Spa's history is recounted in the individual numbered entries which follow, but overall, the Second World War was to leave an indelible mark, bringing famous airmen, military commanders and even King George VI himself to Woodhall Spa. Today, the Spa element is restored at the Golf Hotel's Aqua Santé Spa, after decades of frustrated initiatives at the increasingly derelict Spa Baths.

The Spa Baths in the mid 20th century

Geographical Features, Flora and Fauna

Woodhall Spa is built on the southern tip of an unusual and valuable area of lowland heathland in which sand, gravel and boulder clay occur to a depth of 10 feet, with layers of limestone and clay below. Gorse, ling, heathers and silver birch occur naturally on this sand-blown terrain. Thick plantations of pine trees in the 19th century have given way to the native oak and beech trees, so that the so called Pinewoods in the heart of the Spa, owned by the Woodland Trust, are increasingly a mixture of various trees interwoven with pathways. Wellingtonia and very rare Sequoia Gigantea trees (right) can be seen near the Kinema in the Woods. Waterloo Wood, a lovely oak wood near Reed's Beck, was planted from acorns sown just after the Battle of Waterloo in order to celebrate Wellington's victory.

Squirrels and Woodpeckers

In the 1950s many brown squirrels could still be seen but, as elsewhere, the grey squirrels

have now taken over. Early in the mornings the occasional muntjac and fox can be seen in the woods, and in spring and summer you may see green and greater-spotted woodpeckers, jays, gold-crests, goldfinches, turtle doves, nightjars, and nightingales, as well as blackbirds, chaffinches, blue and great tits, robins, tree-creepers and green finches. Over farmland, there are lapwings and barn-owls. The River Witham flows beneath Kirkstead Bridge to the west of the village, and heron, mallard, teal, mute swans, kingfishers and gulls are common.

So many different types of mushroom and funghi are to be seen around the woods and golf courses that organised trails are sometimes led by experts. In early spring the displays of daffodils and snowdrops along the lanes and notable on the Stixwould Road, are often breathtaking, while in May, the rhododendrons in the Petwood Grounds have become a local legend.

The Woodhall Spa Waters

Many printed accounts of the chemical constituents of the Spa waters have appeared in the local press for many decades. In 1885 it was reckoned to be the strongest Natural Bromine and Iodine Water in Europe. In the 1960s the Spa's Official guide declared that the chemical composition had never varied since it was originally discovered.

The 1952 analysis by Dr. JV Wilson MRCP was:

	Mg per N	/1000 litre
Ammonium	3.4	0.21
Potassium	38.4	0.98
Calcium	525.0	26.25
Chloride	13490.9	380.03
Iodide	6.0	0.05
Bicarbonate	207.4	3.40
Sodium	7590.0	330.0
Magnesium	319.5	26.63
Iron	3.1	0.16
Bromine	38.0	0.48
Silicate	22.1	0.28

An early comparative analysis of Bromine and Iodine in the Spas of Woodhall, Kreuznach, Leamington and Cheltenham revealed that Woodhall's water was very much higher in those substances.

Part Two
Where to go for information

Opened in May 1987, this delightful museum was originally a pre-fabricated structure by Boulton & Paul of Norwich, initially erected on the moor by the Spa's Doctor Cuffe and Stafford Hotchkin, on land now occupied by the Hotchkin Golf Course, in 1884. It is a most unusual survivor of its type. Exactly one century elapsed between the bungalow's arrival on its present site in 1887, and its transformation into Woodhall Spa's community museum. Thomas Wield and his wife Mary worked at the Spa Baths, but their son John worked in the family Bath Chair business, and, as a trained engineer, he made precision instruments and cameras. His photographs form the core of the museum's collection and record events, buildings and people in the history of the Spa between c.1900 and 1965, when he died. Outbuildings included stabling for the donkeys that drew the Bath Chairs, a forge, and photographic darkrooms. In 1985 David Radford was offered the Wield photographs and other memorabilia, by Richard Porter, a much respected dentist in Woodhall, who asked only that a home could be found for their display. Acting as the catalyst for the project, David and a dedicated team purchased the bungalow with the help of a donor who has done much for the area, and by 1987 the Cottage Museum was born.

The Woodhall Spa Cottage Museum Trust was formed in April 1986. It is not commercially based and raises its own finances by fundraising – it is now a Charitable Company limited by Guarantee.

• Local tourist information and souvenirs.
Open Good Friday to the end of October,
Mon – Fri : 10.00am – 5.00pm
Sat – Sun : 10.30 am – 4.30pm
Tel: 01526 353775

The Woodhall Spa Carved Signposts

Four superb carved and painted signs announce Woodhall Spa on each of its four approach roads. They were carved in 1991 by Michael Czajkowski of E Czajkowski & Son, local craftsmen in wood who are devoted to the Spa and its history. The one on Stixwould Road, just past the entrance to the Petwood Hotel as you come into the village, shows the pit and winding gear of 1811 which failed to deliver the coal on which John Parkinson had set his hopes but flooded with the waters which eventually became the Spa waters high in bromine and iodine. A contented cow is seen drinking this beneficial water. The sign on the Tattershall Road shows the nearby Kirkstead Abbey ruin which is in a field to the left, and a monk. The Horncastle Road sign shows the nearby Tower on the Moor, the 15th century hunting tower which can be glimpsed behind bungalows on the right as you drive into the village, and the Witham road sign shows a beautiful steam engine on the old railway which once passed by on the right hand side.

The Parish Council, which commissioned the signs, has enhanced the experience of visitors by providing several metal story boards on sites of interest, by the crossroads at Chapman's Corner and in Royal Square opposite, and in the lovely garden by the Police Station. Two large and colourful plans of the Spa are situated near the Police Station and at Chapman's Corner. The local Rotary Club have provided funding and practical help for many such initiatives in the Spa.

Richard Adolphus Came
the architect of Woodhall Spa Village

Came's Tower in the Royal Hotel Grounds. —

Richard Adolphus Came was born on St. George's Day, 1847, in London. He was educated at Lancing, London and Germany, and was articled to the distinguished architect Sir Matthew Digby Wyatt, who assisted Brunel to design Paddington Station. Wyatt was the official architect of the India Office, and in the 1850s had designed a model village in Swindon for railway workers on the Great Western Railway. No doubt Came was able to study this project before he began his own practice in 1871, firstly in Great James Street, London, and then at Mecklenburg Square, where he was established when the Woodhall Spa syndicate invited him to design a model village. In 1890 he moved to Woodhall Spa, staying first at the Eagle Lodge Hotel, then at his own Royal Hotel in a flat, then in his own home at 'Heatherlea', with his wife Caroline Isabella and his sons and daughters. One son, Kenneth Rex, was accidentally killed in South Africa in 1924, and a daughter, Winifred Mary, died in 1895 in her 17th year, and was buried in Highgate catacombs. R.A. Came died

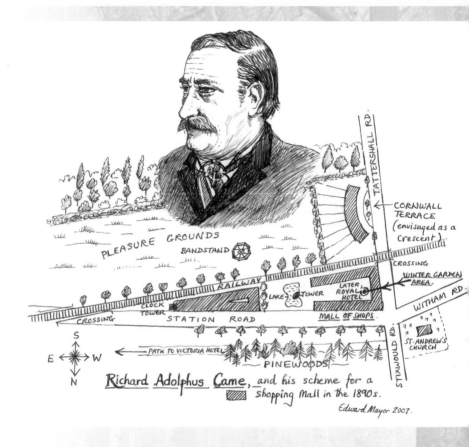

PLEASURE GROUNDS
BANDSTAND

CORNWALL
TERRACE
(envisaged as a crescent)

TATTERSHALL RD.

CROSSING

WINTER GARDEN AREA.

RAILWAY

LATER,
ROYAL
HOTEL

LAKE   TOWER

WITHAM RD.

CLOCK
TOWER

CROSSING

STATION   ROAD

MALL OF SHOPS

STIXWOULD RD.

ST. ANDREW'S
CHURCH

S
E ← W
N

PATH TO VICTORIA HOTEL

PINEWOODS

Richard Adolphus Came, and his scheme for a shopping mall in the 1890s.

Edward Mayor 2007.

in 1917, and his widow lived on in Woodhall Spa, no doubt sharing with Lady Weigall the grief over the death of their daughters while still teenagers. Came achieved the recognition of a fellowship of the Royal Institute of British Architects. Signing his work with panels of over-fired bricks from kiln linings, he effectively transplanted a Bavarian type of architectural detailing to Woodhall Spa and gave his village a distinctly Medieval-German appearance.

Part Three
Vanished Woodhall

Please Note:
Asterisked* places or names are mentioned elsewhere in the guide

The bandstand

Today, the maturity of Woodhall Spa's woodlands tends to compensate for the fact that so much of the original Spa has vanished. Looking towards the Kinema in the Woods, it is impossible to believe that manicured lawns with floral borders, turnstiles and sports facilities, and a grand bandstand once stood on the left, while behind you stood the immense Victoria Hotel. To the right, a large verandah was once attached to the Spa Baths. Then, as paths led from the hotel westwards, the Victorian and Edwardian visitors could go to church at St. Andrew's * by the main crossroads. Today only the leafy graveyard and the walks remain. Fortunately, old postcards and the photographs by John Wield at the Cottage Museum, enable us to reconstruct a leisured age.

The Victoria Hotel

Victoria Hotel and original Spa Baths and Pump Room, commissioned by Thomas Hotchkin, in the late 1830s, were handsome neo-classical stone buildings with portico entrances and tall windows. The hotel had several wings and a coach house, with stabling. In the late 1880s a syndicate of local MPs * injected capital into the Spa and erected the new Bandstand (which stood initially between the Bath House and the Hotel) and a multi-purpose pavilion which became the Kinema *. The bandstand was a copy of the one in South Kensington Gardens. Bath's city architect, Major Davis, remodelled the bath house and Robey's of Lincoln supplied new machinery to raise 20,000 gallons of spa water per day. In 1887 the Pleasure Grounds were laid out by Mr. Dolby of Boston, on what used to be an old cricket field. In the

The Victoria Hotel

1930s, the Weigalls of Petwood converted part of these grounds into a formal Italian Garden with a pool where the bandstand had been. If you visit the woods in the Petwood grounds you can glimpse straight rows of trees to the south of the drainage channel. They are the only reminder of the Italian gardens apart from the overgrown stones of the octagonal pool. In 1888, the same year that the Pleasure Gardens were opened to the public, the Victoria Hotel received another new wing. German aristocrats were now flocking to the Spa and staying in the hotel.

The Victoria Hotel, after the fire in 1920

Fire and Decline

By 1906, the Victoria Hotel had 150 rooms. Tragically, after a redecoration in time for the new season, the hotel burned down in the early hours of Easter Sunday 1920, as a result of an electrical fault in the boiler room. The Weigalls, about to leave for Australia, offered Petwood House as a temporary hotel, and on their return in 1922, bought the Spa Baths and the ruins of the Victoria Hotel, and used the bricks and stone to boon up pathways. Despite their efforts, the 20th century saw several closures and rescues of the Spa Baths, by the Weigalls themselves, by an entrepreneur from Knightsbridge called John Lewis, and by syndicates. Then in 1948 the Lincoln Hospital Group took the Baths on as a rheumatism clinic, and you can still see an old sign to the clinic at the junction of Coronation Road and King George Avenue. The end came unexpectedly on September 21st 1983, when the well lining collapsed inwards, causing a forceful jet of water to shoot up and further demolish other structures.

The Tea House in the Woods

A postcard of the Teahouse dated 1903

This charming café was the very essence of Woodhall Spa as many remember it. The present building on the site, to the south of the old Baths complex, retains a reminder of the old verandah and is now a restaurant. The original chalet was a pretty sight, and was probably erected circa 1900. A dated postcard showing the Teahouse in 1903 would suggest the earlier date, rather than that given by some authorities to be 1907 or 1908. Dr. Williams, Lady Weigall's doctor and the Spa physician who lived in the house next door to the Spa buildings, had two sisters who would come up from London each season to run their teahouse and sell their embroideries and other gifts. They also ran a lending library in the Teahouse. No doubt they are depicted on many postcards showing guests being served!

~ The Teahouse in the Woods in the 1950s ~   E.R.Mayor 2007

A sketch of the Teahouse in the 1950s by Edward Mayor

The Royal Hydro Hotel and Winter Gardens, & Shopping Mall

While the architect Richard Adolphus Came was staying in the Eagle Lodge Hotel,* he designed a magnificent quadrangular shopping mall on the wedge of land bounded by the railway, Tattershall Road, and Station Road. Once this was built, Came responded to calls for a Winter Garden (enabling out of season activities) by building the Royal Hotel in 1897 and provided a fully glazed Winter Garden spanning the area formed by the quadrangle of shops. He had the necessary latticed structures pre-fabricated in Germany but the metal cross-bars were cut to size in the smithy on Witham Road. Proceeding eastwards, he created gardens with ponds and tennis courts, and the grand focal point was the tall medieval German-looking water tower which had been part of his original scheme

The Royal Hotel

The Winter Gardens: The Novelist and mystic Marie Corelli, regarded them as the finest of their kind

and which enabled a panoramic overview of his scheme for Woodhall Spa and the surrounding countryside. In the Second World War, somewhat truncated, it was used for firewatching.

An Alternative Spa

In 1905, Came successfully drilled for the Spa Waters on a site near Cromwell Avenue. Immediately, he built a hydrotherapy wing onto the hotel, and from then on it was called the Royal Hydro Hotel. Many concerts, fetes and dances were held in the Winter Gardens, which had a superb dance floor. Well known entertainers from London gave variety shows and all the local bands appeared. Otherwise the 1920s brought a depression to the Spa, and a Methodist called Mr. Scott-Targett was persuaded to take the hotel on as a temperance hotel. He introduced several facilities for the youth of the village and ran the hotel until it was bombed in 1943.

Widespread Devastation

On the night of the 17th/18th August 1943, the Royal Hotel took two direct hits from German bombs which also damaged the first four houses on Cornwall Terrace (another of Came's schemes). Across Tattershall Road it destroyed 'Chapman's Corner'. Several people were killed, but most of the soldiers billeted in the hotel were away that night. Glass was blown out of most windows on the Broadway. The hotel was flattened so Mr. Scott-Targett presented the site to the village to redevelop as gardens. But a whole way of life had been wiped out, and it is fortunate that the Cottage Museum and the Mall Tavern have many photographs of how Came's grand schemes looked in their heyday.

Chapman's Corner
(corner of Tattershall Road with Witham Road)

Next door to the present hardware store stood a notable store which once supplied the boarding houses and hotels of the Spa with quality goods and foodstuffs from abroad including hams from Denmark and Canada. Chapman & Son, London and Manchester Stores, Established 1845 afterwards became Cargill's, then Basil Kirkby's Ladies & Gentleman's

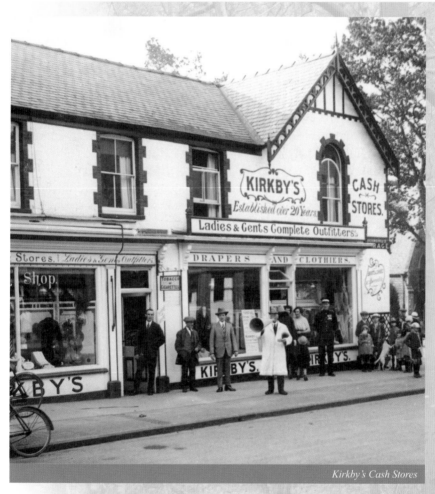

Kirkby's Cash Stores

Complete Outfitters. The bombs which destroyed the Royal Hotel opposite also destroyed this site. Today a large tourist Map of the Spa and a fascinating information plaque feature in a small garden on the site.

The Spa Hotel (Iddesleigh Road)

The hotel stood on the grounds now occupied by the Spa Court apartments. The building began as the 'Northcote Hydro', run by Dr. Cuffe, the licensee of the Spa Baths from 1857 to 1883, then became the Goring Hotel, but Goring and many of the guests were German and had to leave at the outbreak of the First World War, when it became the Lawson Hotel. Then in the 1920s it became the Spa Hotel, much loved by many local people.

The Spa Hotel, when it was called the Lawson Hotel

St. Andrew's Church (at the Woodhall Spa Crossroads)

Built mainly from stone taken from Stixwould priory, the church was founded in 1846 and a village school was built next to it in 1847. The school became a garden centre and is now a handsome private residence, but the church suffered from the blast of the landmine that destroyed the

St Andrew's Church, formerly in the large parish of Langton

Royal Hotel and several houses and shops diagonally opposite in August 1943 and had to be demolished in 1957.

Photographs of the interior show fine poppy-headed pews, carved stone-supports for the roof beams, and carved angels hovering overhead. The arms of the Reverend E Walker and his wife and of the Dymoke and Hotchkin families were carved on some of the roof supports. The extent and the position of the church are discernable in the graveyard, and a handsome curved stone seat memorial to Richard Adolphus Came, Woodhall Spa's main architect is not to be missed.

The Came Memorial

The Vanished Bandstands

Victoria Hotel Orchestra conductor Meyer van Praag.

The Rustic Bandstand

After the octagonal bandstand between the Spa Baths and the Victoria Hotel had been moved to the centre of the lawns of the Pleasure grounds to the west of the Kinema, a rectangular rustic bandstand was erected in its place and various orchestras would play between the two. Messrs. Charles Allen, Meyer van Praag, and the composer Joseph Holbrooke were three of the notable conductors. A third large bandstand once stood in a meadow on the north side of Victoria avenue, flanking the railway and visible (and audible!) from Came's Mall and Gardens. Today the meadow is occupied by houses and gardens.

- Have you spotted a fourth bandstand, the only one remaining today?

Tasburgh Lodge

Tasburgh Lodge on the corner of Victoria Avenue with Stanhope Avenue, shared the same fate as the Royal Hotel complex, being bombed on the night of 17th/18th August 1943. Purpose built as a Doctor's house for Dr. Gwyn, of the Royal Hotel's Spa Baths, it was named after the Norfolk village of Tasburgh, where Dr. Gwyn came from. In 1951 it was rebuilt to an entirely new design and is still a surgery.

The Railway

In order to reconstruct the railway in the mind's eye, stand on the spur of the pavement at the top of Clarence Road with Station Road, and, looking down Clarence Road, you can see where the line came up from Woodhall Junction and across a level crossing on Tattershall Road. Turning exactly 180°, you will then see a wedge-shaped shop on the left of the Broadway,

In the late Victorian period the 'Woodhall Wedge' shop by the old railway station was Overton's Auctioneers and Valuers

just beyond the Police Station and the entrance to a car park. The station occupied that car park, and one of its platforms ran along the back of the Broadway's row of shops, beginning with 'the wedge' as it is called. Local organisations have constructed a small garden next to the Police Station, where you can see a stretch of railway aligning with the direction of the original line.

The railway between Boston and Lincoln opened in 1848, and a branch line between Kirkstead and Horncastle opened in 1855. With the growth

of the Spa, a new station was created at Woodhall Spa in 1888, with a bookshop, and even a lending library. Kirkstead Junction was re-named Woodhall Junction in the 1920s and a through-carriage from London to Woodhall was included on trains leaving King's Cross at 4.00pm. In 1923 the LNER took over the line. In July 1952, an average of 21 passengers were using the service daily, so the passenger service was axed, despite local protests, in 1954. Goods trains continued on to Horncastle until the railway closed completely in April 1971.

Part Four
Woodhall Today

The Golf Courses (1) & (2)

Woodhall Spa is officially the National Golf Centre, and has been famous for golf since 1920. The Woodhall Spa Golf Club was formed in 1891 and golf was played on a nine hole course at 'Mr. Copping's Field' on Tattershall Road. This was succeeded by a second course, also of nine holes which adjoined the old Spa Pleasure Grounds and partly occupied the ground to the south of the Petwood Hotel's raised terrace.

The Hotchkin Course (1)

This is one of the finest courses in the world and has frequently appeared in America's 'Golf Magazine' in the top 50. Currently it is ranked at 53rd. The most recent issues of UK magazine 'Golf World' declare the Hotchkin to be the finest Inland course in the UK and the ninth best overall in the UK. With roughly 3500 courses in Britain and Northern Ireland the Hotchkin's rankings are enviable, and it is not surprising that the English

Golf Union made its headquarters here in 1995 buying the course, Club House and outbuildings, and 180 acres of land around Bracken Wood for a second course which opened on May 22nd 1998.

Contrasting Courses

The Bracken Course

In 1905, Stafford Vere Hotchkin, Lord of the Manor, gave 150 acres of family land known on old maps as 'The Moor', for an eighteen hole golf course. Designed by Harry Vardon with some input by J.H. Taylor, it was altered and extended in 1912, and redesigned by Colonel S.V. Hotchkin in the early 1920s, receiving accolades from top players and reporters. The sandy heath land enabled the excavation of deep and challenging bunkers, and the course cleverly accommodated the railway line to Horncastle and part of the Viking Way, which in the early days was simply a public pathway with no name. Heather and deep bunkers are the principle hazards of the Hotchkin, whereas the Bracken course has wide fairways, shallow bunkers and undulating greens, being constructed on clay, which makes deep bunkers impossible. Many of its greens have been built up around lakes, irrigation channels and stands of ancient lime coppice, and a dramatic avenue, seemingly cut through trees and going uphill towards the Bracken course from the Hotchkin is thought to be the line of a roman road, with clay pits for Roman kilns near Monument Road being turned into lakes. Fine views can be obtained from the pathway skirting the Petwood Estate and from Manor Road (see Walk 2)

Statistics for two great courses

All major amateur championships have been held at Woodhall Spa, which currently lacks the infrastructure needed for professional tournaments. Regardless of what the future may hold, Woodhall Spa is the home of English Golf, and its contrasting courses (The Bracken planned by Donald Steel) test different skills. There is also a twenty bay floodlit Driving Range, a 3.7 acre short game area, and two-day golf schools between April and September.

Hotchkin Course
From the championship tees, the course measures 7087 yards and is par 73. From the general play tees it measures 6500 yards and is par 71.

Bracken Course
From the championship tees, the course measures 6735 yards and is par 72. From the general play tees it measures 6189 yards and is par 72.

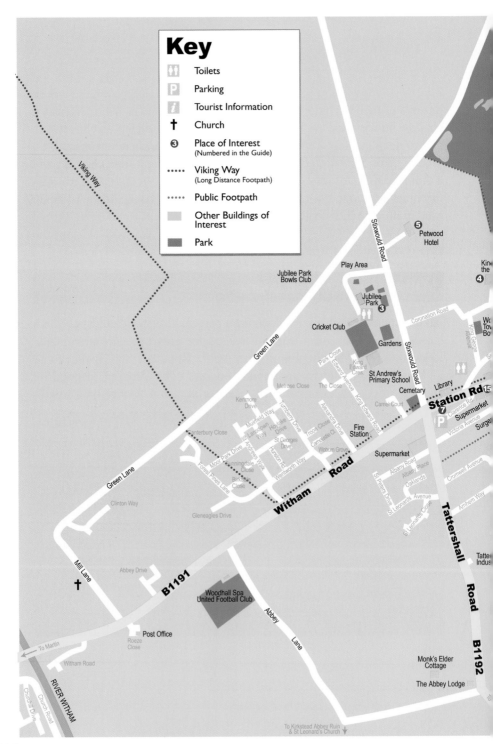

Key

	Toilets
P	Parking
i	Tourist Information
†	Church
❸	Place of Interest (Numbered in the Guide)
·····	Viking Way (Long Distance Footpath)
·····	Public Footpath
	Other Buildings of Interest
	Park

Viking Way

Slixwould Road

❺ Petwood Hotel

Play Area

Jubilee Park Bowls Club

Kin· the

❹

Coronation Road

Wo Tow Bo

Cricket Club

Jubilee Park ❸

Gardens

Slixwould Road

King George Avenue

Green Lane

Park Close

King Edward Avenue

St Andrew's Primary School

Cemetery

Library

Station Rd

❼ P

Supermarket

Surger

Melrose Close

The Close

King Edward Road

Carmel Court

Clarence Rd

Kenmore Drive

Munfield Way

Lansdown Way

Canterbury Close

Ansbury Drive

Honville Drive

Alexandra Drive

St Georges Drive

Troon Close

Carnoustie Cl

Wentworth Way

Fire Station

Webburn Grove

Moor Park Drive

Andrew Walk

Turnburg Rd

Victoria Avenue

Sunningdale Close

Birkdale Close

Forest Pines Lane

Supermarket

Albany Road

Albany Place

Oaklands

Cromwell Avenue

Arnhem Way

Green Lane

Clinton Way

Gleneagles Drive

Witham Road

St Peters Drive

St Leonards Avenue

St Leonards Close

Tattershall

Tatte Indus

Mill Lane

Abbey Drive

B1191

Woodhall Spa United Football Club

Road

B1192

†

To Martin

Roeze Close

Post Office

Witham Road

Abbey Lane

Monk's Elder Cottage

The Abbey Lodge

RIVER WITHAM

Church Road

Churchill Drive

To Kirkstead Abbey Ruin & St Leonard's Church ▼

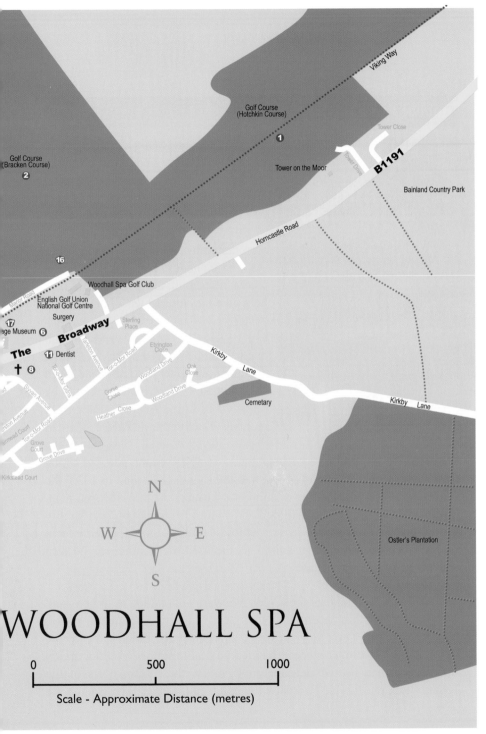

Viking Way

Golf Course
(Hotchkin Course)
❶

Tower Close

Tower Drive

B1191

Golf Course
(Bracken Course)
❷

Tower on the Moor

Bainland Country Park

Horncastle Road

16

Woodhall Spa Golf Club

Manor Road

English Golf Union
National Golf Centre

Surgery

Sterling
Place

⑰

ⓐge Museum ⑥

Broadway

Ebrington
Close

Kirkby

Lane

The

⑪ Dentist

Iddesleigh Avenue

Tor-o-Mor Road

Oak
Close

✝ ⑧

Tor-o-Mor Gardens

Woodland Drive

Kirkby

Lane

Gorse
Close

Woodland Drive

Cemetery

Sixten Avenue

Heather Close

armead Court

rston Avenue

Tor-o-Mor Road

Grove
Court

Grove Drive

Kirkstead Court

N
W · E
S

Ostler's Plantation

WOODHALL SPA

0   500   1000

Scale - Approximate Distance (metres)

37

The park was originally a large pleasure garden laid out by Lady Grace Weigall for the many charity events and weekend house parties which the Weigalls held from Petwood House on the other side of Stixwould Road. A long pool was surrounded by an extensive paved area, stone colonnades, pergolas and lawns where afternoon tea parties could be held on a massive scale.

The Weigalls were friendly with many members of the Royal family, and their daughter Priscilla had been a Debutante. The gardens could be regarded as Lady Weigall's attempt to recreate Buckingham Palace Garden Parties in Woodhall Spa, and the Weigalls had in mind a second spa baths complex on the site, for which their friend Princess Marie-Louise laid the foundation stone in 1935, the Jubilee year of King George V and Queen Mary. At the same moment, it was declared the 'Royal Jubilee Park' should from then on be a facility for the people of Woodhall Spa to enjoy…. but the grand scheme for a second spa came to nothing and today the foundation stone can be seen in the base of the park's café.

In 1947, the Weigalls in their old age were unloading as much land and property as they could, and had been living at Englemere, Ascot, for many years. Thus they presented their 'Royal Jubilee Park' to the local council, and ever since it has featured a variety of outdoor sports activities with a heated outdoor pool, and is the headquarters of the Tennis Club, the Jubilee Park Bowling Club (the 'Town' Bowls Club are established on King George Avenue) and the Croquet Club, with cycle hire facilities in the season, a children's playground, a caravan park, a putting green, toilets, bandstand and gravelled walks with pergolas and floral lawns. The park lends a festive atmosphere to Woodhall Spa throughout the year and is beautifully maintained.

In 1951 Sir Archibald Weigall returned to Woodhall Spa and to Jubilee Park, to open the new children's pool and told his audience that people had thought his late wife quite mad to erect classical columns on such a forlorn heath land in preparation for her park, but she told them to return in a year or two and see how the flower beds were flourishing and the roses growing up the columns. Lady Weigall's dream has turned into a virtual inland resort and today there are big plans to improve the heated pool and café.

Meanwhile the Woodhall Spa Cricket Club on its adjacent grounds next to the park is improving social facilities for its members, and the croquet club is also expanding its activities.

The Kinema in the Woods (4)

THE KINEMA IN THE WOODS AT WOODHALL SPA.

Featured many times on radio and TV, the core of this famous building was erected in 1888 as a pavilion in which dancing, theatricals, fetes and village meetings could be held. With a verandah facing the new pleasure grounds (now thick woodland) it doubled as a sports pavilion, then in August 1922 the Weigalls of nearby Petwood House, turned it into a cinema.

Rear Projection
Large cross beams supporting the roof did not allow an image to be projected from the rear of the hall, so a long hut was erected at the back of the building, enabling the image to be back-projected some 30 feet onto a translucent screen. This arrangement, now thought to be unique in this country, has been continually upgraded with new projectors and screens.

Changes of Name
Originally called 'The Pavilion Cinema' it was given its present name by C.C. Allport, the man who ran it for over 50 years from 1922. In 1930 he had announced the coming of the 'talkies' and renamed the place 'The Kinema In The Woods' after the Greek KINE or 'motion' used for thousands of Kinemas at the time.

Deckchairs
Until the 1950s, the first few rows of seats were wide deckchairs, occupied by many famous guests and even royalty in the shape of Princess Marie-Louise. Thousands of servicemen and women stationed in the area during the Second World War watched films in their beloved 'Flicks in The Sticks' as they called it. After the War, a Polish artist and ex-serviceman, Nickolai Kukso, painted murals for the new foyer and marbling in the auditorium, which still exist, and in his youth the film director Bryan Forbes made many visits to the Kinema.

Changes Under New Ownership
C.C. Allport died in 1973 and the Kinema was sold to James Green, who bought and installed the famous Compton Kinestra organ in 1987. Rescued from a London cinema, the organ was built by John Compton

to sound like an orchestra, and is today the only survivor of three. James Green's many other improvements include a new foyer and in 1994 a second screen, Kinema Too, with murals of Lincolnshire and a portrait of Major Allport by Canadian Artist Murray Hubick. Hubick also painted in trompe l'oeil two panels inside the main auditorium.

DON'T MISS
- The displays of cinema memorabilia, old projectors, and postcards of Old Woodhall Spa in the foyer
- The Memory Lane Shows with live organ music and clips from old movies
- Can you spot an umbrella and raincoat which could never be used in the rain?

The Petwood Hotel (5)

Petwood House as redesigned by Frank Peck, c.1920

This magnificent House was built for a Baroness in the throes of a divorce, in 1905. She had fallen in love with the woodland at the Spa while staying at the Victoria Hotel, and she referred to it as her 'pet wood'. The Baroness Von Eckhardstein was Sir Blundell Maple's only surviving daughter and she filled this 'Arts & Crafts' style half-timbered house with Maple's furniture, but its superb oak staircase was designed by Frank Peck, the architect who altered Petwood considerably after the now divorced Grace Maple married Captain (later Sir) Archibald Weigall, in 1910. Peck's stated purpose was to create a Jacobean-seeming house, and the gardens were laid out by Harold Peto, the great exponent of the Italianate garden and admirer of Gertrude Jeckyll, whose plantings he imitated. From 1910 to 1920 the Weigalls entertained lavishly, welcoming royalty, local aristocracy, many children – and many cricket teams!

Colourful Changes

In 1922 the Weigalls returned from a spell in South Australia where Sir Archibald had been Governor, and found Woodhall Spa in a depressed state, so Grace decide to open a cinema in the old Pavilion they had just acquired. Tax problems caused them to relinquish Petwood towards 1934, but they helped their friends John and Peggy Flury to refurbish and open it as an hotel. A great success, it was then requisitioned as an Officers' Mess in 1943 for some locally based squadrons (notable 617, the Dambusters, from RAF Scampton). The Petwood re-opened as an hotel in 1945, and since the 1960s, it has experienced many changes of ownership, but is now in private hands again, and so successful that a vast new suite, the Woodland Suite, was added in 2004. Famous visitors over its 100 year history have included King George VI when a young prince, Princess Marie-Louise, Eugenie Queen of Spain, Gracie Fields, Guy Gibson, Leonard Cheshire, Prince Charles, and a host of aristocratic, sporting and media celebrities and film stars.

The Squadron Bar at the Petwood

DON'T MISS
- The famous Squadron Bar with its memorabilia of 617 Squadron's campaigns
- The grounds, with Grace Weigall's own woods and the remains of several formal gardens, with dazzling Rhododendron displays each May.
- In the forecourt, one of the remaining prototype 'bouncing bombs' invented by Barnes Wallis for the Dambusters raid.

The Golf Hotel (6)

Built in 1888, this striking climax to The Broadway is now the home of Woodhall's Spa. With the original Spa complex currently in limbo, Mr. Narendra Patel took the opportunity to put the Spa back into Woodhall, and engaged North Sea drillers to obtain the bromo-iodine waters for the new Aqua Santé Spa, which opened on October 3rd 2005. It is hoped that two further pools and some 40 treatment rooms will in the near future create one of the finest active Spas in the world and rival the excellence of the local golf courses.

'Clevedon', as the original 'highly half-timbered' building was called, was probably designed by R.A. Came and was made into 'the Clevedon House Preparatory School for Boys', run by Ernest Stokoe, MA, founded years earlier, and with an initial enrolment of only two pupils. Once lit throughout by acetylene gas, the present hotel retains a robust reminder of the old days, in the gents' toilets.

T.P. Stokoe, Ernest's brother, next ran the building (c.1912) as the 'Clevedon Club for Gentlemen', and some locals remember it as the Clevedon Hotel, but it became the Golf Hotel in the spring of 1921, no doubt reflecting the Stokoe brothers' involvement in local golf, and filling the gap left by the destruction of the Victoria Hotel by fire in 1920. It is likely that the present entrance, bars, lounge and east wing were added at, or shortly after, this time. The wood panelling, open-plan feel, and golfing memorabilia bring distinction to the interior.

- The date of the original building is carved in an unusual place. Can you spot it?
- To the west of the Golf Hotel at the corner of Iddesleigh Road and the Broadway, is Longwood House, said to be a replica of Napoleon's house of exile on St. Helena, which was also called Longwood. The verandah is apparently the only similar feature. Longwood was a Special treatment Establishment at one time, under the direction of F. Hardy. You could have 'Plombiere Massages' and Modern Electrical treatments there. In earlier years this lovely house rejoiced in the name 'Oranienhof'!

Royal Square and the Dambuster's Memorial (7)

The Square was presented to the Urban District Council of Woodhall Spa by members of the Woodhall Spa Royal Hotel and Winter Gardens Limited, whose property on the site was damaged by enemy action on the night of 17th-18th August 1943, so that a space could be created 'for the

ROYAL SQUARE, WOODHALL SPA

benefit of the public'. The resulting square is now dominated by the majestic Dambuster's Memorial in the form of a breached dam with water pouring from its centre. It commemorates the men of 617 Squadron who died in operations between 1943-45. The memorial site was donated by East Lindsey District Council and the inscriptions on the side read:

'erected by the comrades of those who died in 1939-'45 and dedicated on May 17th 1987 .... 204 aircrew were sacrificed'.

And the architect, K. Stevens ARIBA, is named alongside the engineer, D.C. Fletcher, and the stonemasons, Leakes of Louth.

A Remarkable Dedication Ceremony

A photographic record proves that during the ceremony, a black dog resembling Guy Gibson's 'Nigger' came to sit calmly in the centre of the choir, then disappeared. Inquiries could not ascertain its ownership. Nigger was killed by a car on the very night when Gibson led the Squadron on its most famous and successful raid on the German dams on the night of May 16th, 1943.

See also THE ROYAL HYDRO HOTEL and WINTER GARDENS.

Places of Worship

St. Peter's Church (C of E) (8)

Designed by Hodgson Fowler and built in 1893 to seat 5 – 600 people, at a cost of just over £2000. A handsome red-brick structure, it was later panelled with wood on its side walls and oak chairs were replaced by pews. Frank Peck, the architect of Petwood House nearby, states on his RIBA admissions document that he did the 'sanctuary arcading' in 1913. In 1930 the present nave and chancel were added to the original building which became the south aisle and Lady Chapel. In 1934 the small bell turret was added. The pulpit was given in memory of T.J. Stafford Hotchkin by his son, and the brass lectern by his widow. The organ is a 2 manual instrument by Jardine & Co of Manchester. Pevsner, in his famous 'Buildings of England, Lincolnshire', says that St. Peter's is 'of a type familiar from wealthy suburbs'! Certainly the East window, by James Powell of London, features not only Christ in Triumph with angels, saint and apostles, but also (and unusually) people like Dante, King Alfred, Piers Plowman, and Thomas Linacre! The Church Hall is next door.

St. Peter's Church

The Roman Catholic Church of Our Lady & St. Peter (9)

Built in 1896 to seat 200 people, the church was established following a mission from Grantham. The architect was R.A. Came, and the builder was Oliver Cromwell. Considering the career of his famous namesake, this has a delicious irony. He even claimed to be a descendant of the Lord Protector. Mr. Cromwell's grave is in St. Andrew's churchyard. Set in beautiful grounds off Cromwell Avenue, the Catholic church itself is modest and plain, unusual for Came, but a superb carved altar with three quatrefoils features two angels flanking the central lilies, nicely painted, and a beautifully executed painting of the Virgin and Child by Polish ex-serviceman and trained artist, Nickolai Kukso, hangs above the lectern. Kukso had a studio at Halstead Hall near Stixwould and executed large decorative paintings at the Kinema in the Woods * and Martin Hall. A majestic glazed porch allowing wheelchair access has just been added by the builders M.J. Green of Navenby and the architects Neil Dowlman Ltd.

Note: R.A. Came also designed an identical Roman Catholic Church in Skegness

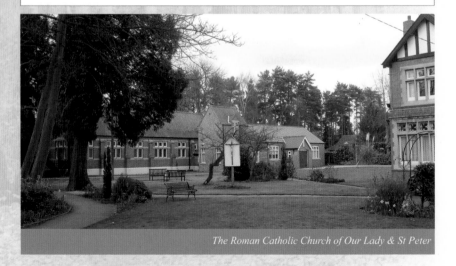

The Roman Catholic Church of Our Lady & St Peter

The Methodist Chapel (10)

It was built on the Broadway in 1907 at a cost of £2,500 to seat 400 people. It replaced the Witham Road chapel, and did so with a tremendous flourish, with a tower and spire by Thompson of Louth. Today this church conducts its worship and other activities in the building to the rear, in the former school room via the Iddesleigh Road entrance. The welcoming and bright chapel thus replaces the original building, which 12 years ago became business premises. All the original panelling and fittings remain.

The Presbyterian (Unitarian) Chapel at Kirkstead on Mill Lane.

Founded in 1694 and built in 1821, this charming red-brick chapel conducts four services a year and sits in a beautiful graveyard. It is also a children's nursery for most of the time, and the toys and projects mingle with the wooden pulpit and memorial tablets to former clergymen.

Tel: 01526 352247 for further details.

Grand Houses and Hotels on the Broadway

The Alexandra Hospital (now private apartments) (11)

Opened on May 29th 1890 by the Countess Brownlow, this handsome building was erected from funds raised in many ways by the Reverend J.O. Stephens of Blankney and his syndicate (see entry on Spa Baths). It was enlarged several times by architects including Frank Peck *. The idea was that people suffering from rheumatic diseases who could not afford to stay in hotels or partake of the Woodhall Spa Baths, would nevertheless receive treatment. Alexandra, Princess of Wales consented to be patron of the hospital. The collapse of the well at the Spa Baths precipitated the closure of the hospital in 1984 after almost a century of treatments.

❖ The Alexandra Hospital ~ a fine essay in Dutch Classicism after several enlargements.

Hartington House (12)

Designed by R.A. Came as a boarding house, it was taken on by Suzannah Lunn of Horncastle as a high school for girls. Miss Lunn was the daughter of a chemist and grocer in Bridge Street, Horncastle, and her brother became Sir Henry Lunn of Lunn's Travel. Miss Lunn retired in 1926 and Hartington House reverted to a boarding house while her successor moved the school over to 'Fairmead' in Stanhope Avenue.

Victoria Lodge (13)

Now a dental studio, is adjacent to Hartington House, and was another guest house which served as an annexe to Miss Lunn's school. During the Second World War, soldiers were billeted there, and many would stream across to the Methodist church opposite on Sundays.

Woodlands (14)

At the corner of Stanhope Avenue and the Broadway, it is today Broadway Carpets and Curtains. But it used to be the home of Dr. Gwyn, and it was also briefly used by St Andrew's Primary School and as an hotel, before being converted to retail. It has variously been an electrical store, an antique shop and a cycle spares centre. It appears to have been an hotel in 1915 when postcards were being sent from there. The present owners of the building have reinstated the superb old ironwork canopies.

The Woodhall Spa Hotel (15)

Eagle Lodge Hotel, Woodhall Spa.

On the opposite corner to Woodlands, was built a home for Charles Blyton in the early 1870s, and called Eagle House. Blyton was a nursery man whose plots were situated by Woodhall Spa station. The building became an hotel in 1882 and was known as the Eagle Lodge Pension Hotel. Catering to the growing demand for visitor accommodation, it was reported to be full to capacity and was enlarged in 1888. During the Edwardian period it was run by a Miss Lamb. It became a nursing home in the late 1960s after the heyday of the Spa, but reopened its doors as the Eagle Lodge Hotel in 1991, until sold to its present owners, Hoby Hotels, who gave it a complete facelift and its present name in 2005.

The Garden Bar has some memorabilia of the exploits of 617 Squadron, but unlike other hotels and guesthouses the hotel was not requisitioned by the army. However, servicemen met socially and 'did their drinking' at the Eagle Lodge Hotel, so it played its part in Woodhall Spa's war.

The Manor House (16) Not open to the public

This imposing red brick house, basically late 18th century with many 19th and 20th century additions, was the home of the Hotchkin family, lords of the Manor. It was for some time the offices of the National Farmers' Union, and was called "Agriculture House", then various businesses have occupied it to the present day.

The Manor House, north elevation

A walled garden shields the house, but there has been an attempt at late Georgian symmetry on the north front, and upstairs the West front reveals sweeping views of 'Hotchkin's Field' now part of the Bracken Golf course, with the breathtaking vista continued from the North front. Inside, superb oak and mahogany panelling abound, and the imposing entrance hall is reached through an arcade of three openings with pilasters. Window seats project from the upstairs corridor windows, and a vast polished wood ingle-nook in the largest downstairs room to the East, displays carved fretwork and roundels repeated in the woodwork of the main door. The aristocratic sweep of the Hotchkin domains can be seen from Manor Road, and puts into perspective the comparatively dazzling extravagance of the Weigall's Petwood House, built largely from the large inherited fortune of the Maple furniture empire.

The Dower House Hotel (17) just down Manor Road a few hundred yards from the Manor House, is described in Walk 2

Places of Interest around Kirkstead

Kirkstead Abbey and the Church of St Leonard

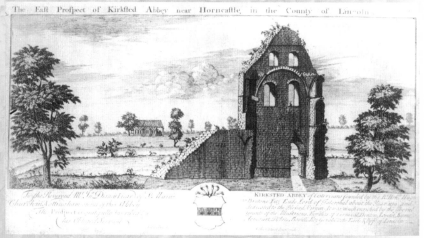

The East Prospect of Kirksted Abbey near Horncastle, in the County of Lincoln

KIRKSTED ABBEY

Kirkstead Abbey, a Daughter-house of Fountains Abbey, was founded in c. 1139 by the Cistercian Hugo de Brito of Tattershall and was moved to its present site in 1187. It became a ruin at the 'Dissolution of the Monasteries' and today only a craggy fragment remains above ground, this being the south east angle of the south transept. Pevsner noted indications of a dormitory and a passage adjoining the transept and opening to the former cloister. A portion of the south wall of the south transept's eastern chapel bears an indication of vaulting. The relatively plain detailing is typical of the Cistercian way of building, as was the site, far from other habitations, but near a river. The monks worked on the land.

St Leonard's Church

St Leonard's Church, just beyond the abbey ruins, has often been described as the chapel "ante portas" or gate chapel of the abbey, but today's archaeological opinion is moving towards it being a Chantry Chapel possibly for Sir Robert de Tateshall who died in 1212, which was perhaps rescued from destruction at the dissolution of the monasteries, by the Clinton family. Architecturally it is a gem, and as Pevsner rightly says, is of 'Cathedral Standard'. The slender columns, carved capitals, rib vaults, dog-tooth ornamentation, lancet windows and original wooden screen, are all superb and point to a date of c. 1230-40. In the chapel's present existence as St Leonard's Church it has a devoted congregation and, unusually, no electricity, so that the atmosphere and acoustic are very special.

Abbey Lodge Inn

NOTE: a cattle grid at the Abbey Lane entrance to the site confirms the presence of grazing cows. Cars can park in the lane going past the ruin toward the church.

The Abbey Lodge Inn at the junction of Abbey Lane with Tattershall Road was once a lodge or gatehouse for the Abbey and its extensive vaulted cellars have now been filled in.

Stone from the Abbey was used to build Abbey Farm and Kirkstead Old Hall, which dates from the 17th century, but the ancient 'mud and stud' method was used to build the picturesque 'Monks Elder Cottage', visible from Abbey Lane opposite the farm and only in winter. It is the only other listed building in the area, apart from THE STATION HOUSE, by Kirkstead Bridge, which is the oldest listed commercial building in the Woodhall Spa area.

Continuing along Witham Road in the direction of Kirkstead Bridge, fork left just before the bridge to see THE RAILWAY HOTEL and STATION HOUSE.

Woodhall Junction

Woodhall Junction including the Station House, was built by the Great Northern Railway in 1848 (see entry in 'Vanished Woodhall'). The Italianate look of the station is echoed at Tattershall and several other stations on the Lincolnshire loop line (Peterborough to Gainsborough). The station became a junction in 1855 when the Horncastle  Railway Company opened its seven mile line, by which time Woodhall Spa had grown enough to justify a small wooden platform and basic facilities for travellers. The station at Kirkstead was at first named Kirkstead Station but became Woodhall Junction in 1922 as part of Sir Archibald Weigall's promotional exercise to bring visitors to Woodhall Spa. Fascinating railway memorabilia can be seen in and around the Station Master's house, which along with the platforms, two goods sheds and the main brick built offices, are all that remain of the station. A biannual open day is sometimes held in September and advertised locally for Heritage Week.

- Many visitors will remember the actor Donald Pleasance. His father was Station Master here, and helped the station to win "Best Kept Station" in 1933
- Please respect the fact that the Station House is a private home. A storyboard outlines the facts, with photographs, next to the platform.

The Railway Hotel. A Mr. Fowler was the first victualler, then a Mr Atkinson, followed by his son. Atkinson Snr. went to California for seven years and made a fortune, but of great interest to the visitor is the fact that he supplied families with 'Genuine Home Brewed Ale'!

Witham Bank Scenic Drive

Proceed over Kirkstead Bridge in the direction of Martin for The Witham Bank Scenic Drive, which is reached by taking the first left turn into the hamlet and keeping left up to the top of the embankment. From this point you will see the Station House opposite and as you drive alongside the wide, meandering River Witham, you will see on your left the Kirkstead Abbey ruins, then shortly afterwards (also on your left) the towers of Tattershall Church and Tattershall Castle.

Meanwhile, cattle and horses graze on the banks, waterfowl and boats enjoy the river, fishing is frequently seen on the bank immediately to your left, and eventually, past several farmsteads and newly built houses on the right, you will see the stunning Timberland Drain (from the bridge and looking right), then, after the turn to Thorpe Tilney, you come to the Timberland Pumping Station built in 1839 to drain 2,500 acres in the Timberland and Thorpe Tilney Fens. There is a 'Tales of the Riverbank' Visitor Centre here, presently closed, but information regarding future

The Timberland Pumping Station

openings can be had from the Sleaford Tourist Information Centre (01529 414294). Meandering onwards with the river taking ever more majestic curves, you arrive at Tattershall Bridge and if you take a left turn into Tattershall you will see the splendid Station House on the right, then the famous Tattershall Castle and Church.

Tattershall Castle and Church of Holy Trinity are linked, for Ralph Cromwell Treasurer of England in 1433, had them, and a college, built in the 1430s. The college premises have gone completely, The first castle was actually built by Sir Robert de Tateshall in the 13th Century. Then in 1445-6, a certain 'Brickmaker Baldwin' supplied 322,000 bricks from his kilns at Edlington Moor, 9 miles north, and Lord Cromwell, whose family had lived at Tattershall since 1367, was able to build the handsome keep we see today.

The Church of the Holy Trinity begun in 1440 was completed by Bishop Waynflete in the 1480s, is 184 ft long, of Ancaster stone, a masterpiece of Perpendicular architecture, and amply glazed. The fine organ is dramatically placed.

Part 5

Local Airfields and Aviation Museums – An RAF tour from Woodhall Spa

Duration: A full two days will be needed

Best Time: ALL SITES open on Wednesdays in July and August. SOME OPEN all year round, so check beforehand with each site. OPENING TIMES MAKE A VISIT TO ALL SITES DESCRIBED HERE POSSIBLE ONLY OVER SEVERAL DAYS.

Despite the fact that the famous air raids on key German Dams took place on May 1943 from Scampton near Lincoln, Woodhall Spa has become famous as the eventual home of the 'Dam busters' 617 Squadron, with its officers based at the Petwood Hotel from January 1944. From RAF Woodhall's airfield near Ostler's Plantation, the Squadron flew to many other successful raids such as that on the Tirpitz Battleship in September 1944. But other squadrons were also based at Woodhall Spa including 97, 619 and the 627 Mosquito Squadron.

Suggested Itinerary, Day One:
Woodhall Spa Dambuster's Memorial - East Kirkby Aviation Heritage Centre - Coningsby Battle of Britain Memorial Flight.

Leave Woodhall Spa after an early breakfast, from Royal Square where the Dambuster's Memorial stands in tranquil gardens and takes the form of a breached dam with water pouring from the centre (Car park (free) next to the square, off Station Road). Proceed down Tattershall Road, noting the sign for RAF Woodhall Spa after about 2 miles on the left. This site is still used in a small way by the RAF, especially as it has a 9 hole golf course. There is also a quarrying site, and when this business closes, that part of the site will be taken on by the Lincolnshire Wildlife Trust. Further on and to the right you will see Thorpe Camp (near Tattershall Thorpe) with its huts where the airmen were billeted (see itinerary, Day Two). Proceed through Coningsby, taking the A155 to Mareham le Fen, then on to Revesby with its beautiful Abbey and Parkland on the left, and finally, still on the A155, arrive at EAST KIRBY.

RAF EAST KIRKBY
THE LINCOLNSHIRE AVIATION HERITAGE CENTRE.
Open all year round, Mon – Sat (summer 9.30am – 5pm, winter 10am – 4pm)
Tel: 01790 763207 – Website www.lincsaviation.co.uk

This was the home of 57 and 630 Squadrons in 5 Group, and features one of only two working Avro Lancaster Bombers in the UK. This Lancaster is not permitted to take-off, unlike the one at the Battle of Britain Memorial Flight, but it does taxi round the airfield, offering rides on Saturdays and Bank Holidays (and full VIP experience on Wednesdays). There is also a resident Spitfire that performs air displays on occasions (check the website for details). The display, memorabilia, shop, café and general welcoming atmosphere are superb and you will certainly need between two and three hours to absorb it all.

Return to Coningsby on the A155 and follow signs south for RAF Coningsby.

THE BATTLE OF BRITAIN MEMORIAL FLIGHT and VISITOR CENTRE
RAF CONINGSBY
Open Mon – Fri, 10am – 5pm, Closed weekends, Bank Holidays and 2 weeks at Christmas and New Year . Tel: 01526 344041 – Website: www.bbmf.co.uk

In 1986 it became possible, thanks to Lincolnshire County Council and the RAF, to view the historic aircraft of the Battle of Britain Memorial Flight at their home base at RAF Coningsby. Now, you can take a guided tour of the BBMF Hangar, with its Lancaster, Spitfires, Hurricanes and Dakota, and in the Visitor Centre there are superb displays, a souvenir shop and small picnic area with hot and cold drinks available (ample free parking facilities). You will need between 2 and 3 hours to absorb the experience. There is also a small viewing and car parking area just further along the road towards Dogdyke, next to the runway. This is an ideal spot to view the many different types of aircraft landing and taking-off from this, once again, very busy airfield. You will see the RAF's latest fighter, the Typhoon, plus all of its other fast jets, Harriers and Tornados, as well as the occasional visiting American jets. The viewing area sometimes has ice creams and drinks for sale in the summer.

Suggested itinerary for another day, ideal for a Sunday, May – Sept.
RAF Digby - RAF Cranwell - RAF Metheringham - and/or Thorpe Camp, Tattershall.

Leaving Woodhall Spa around 10am, proceed outwards on the B1191 through Martin, and turn left at the junction with the B1189. On the B1189, take the first right turn to Scopwick, and at Scopwick, turn right, then left for Digby, on the B1191.

RAF Digby, Lima Sector Operations Room Museum

Open every Sunday, May to September, with a single, free, guided tour at 11am. There is no need to pre-book, simply turn up at the free parking spot in the sports field car park opposite the Main Gate, but be early because the guide will meet you there shortly before 11am and escort you onto the station. The operations room has been restored to its World War II appearance and has plotting tables and State Boards, a large photographic collection, and a restored 'Pipsqueak Table' used to plot friendly fighters. For more guided tour details ring the Visit Coordinator on 01526 327619 or the Sleaford Tourist Information Centre on 01529 414294 – Website: www.raf.mod.uk/rafdigby

Cranwell Aviation Heritage Centre.

From RAF Digby, take the B1191 westwards to the junction with the A15 and turn left, noting after a few miles the right turn to Cranwell, and North Rauceby, where you will find the Cranwell Aviation Heritage Centre. Open: Wednesdays, Thursdays and Sundays 10.30am – 4.30 pm May to September (also Bank Holiday Mondays). Tel: 01529 488940 or Sleaford Tourist Information Centre 01529 414294. There are photographs, exhibits and archive film portraying Cranwell's history, and there is a computerised flight simulator, a Vampire T.11 XE946 and a Jet Provost T4. Parking and entry is free and there is also a souvenir shop.

106 Squadron Visitor Centre, RAF Metheringham.

From Cranwell Aviation Heritage Centre, return north on the A15, branch right onto the B1191, then right onto the B1188, then left to Scopwick,

after which, turn left onto the B1189 until you reach the right turn to Martin and Woodhall Spa where you will need to turn left down a lane opposite this junction for the Visitor Centre.

Open Easter to October, Wednesdays 12 Noon to 4pm; Sundays and Bank Holidays 12 Noon – 5pm – Tel: 01526 378270
Website: www.metheringhamairfield.org

During 1942, around 600 acres of farmland and woodland were cleared to create the airfield for No. 5 Group Bomber Command, which opened in October 1943, in time for the Battle of Berlin. The airfield closed in spring 1946, returning to agriculture, however there is now a Visitor Centre at West Moor Farm. The former Ration Store has been restored and houses a fascinating exhibition of photographs and Memorabilia recording life on an operational Second World War airfield. There is a souvenir shop at the centre and the memorial to 106 Squadron is on the airfield nearby.

Thorpe Camp Visitor Centre, Tattershall Thorpe.
Finally, on Sundays from Easter to the end of September, and on Wednesdays during July and August (open 2-5pm) –
Website: www.thorpecamp.org.uk

The Thorpe Camp Visitor Centre is the closest airfield attraction to Woodhall Spa. Take the Tattershall Road (B1192) from Woodhall Spa, and arrive in five minutes at the camp, which is on the right of a bend. An English Electric Lightening aircraft is on display outside, and photographs and memorabilia are on show inside. The huts, some hidden by woodland, were occupied by the men of 617 and 69 Squadrons.

Walk 1

The Old Residential Area and Shopping Centre

(Allow 1 ½ hours for a stroll – can be muddy in one section of the route)

Leaving Royal Square on the Tattershall Road, imagine the railway crossing where you see the pathway on the left. Glancing across at the supermarket, imagine a nursery once flanking the railway line which went to Kirkstead. Proceeding down Tattershall Road you see on the left a fine terrace of houses conceived by the Spa's architect R.A. Came in the 1890s. Cornwall Terrace was drawn as a Crescent on his plan, but materialised

Long Avenue

as a rectangular block with a diagonal corner projection. Cross over the junction with Victoria Avenue, noting that several other Came houses are on the Avenue, including 'Sylvanhay'. Continue along Tattershall road and turn left down Long Avenue, a pathway between the backs of long gardens, very muddy in some areas but leafy and relaxing. Eventually, on your right, go through a gateway leading immediately to the Roman Catholic Church and its attendant buildings situated picturesquely on lawns leading through to Cromwell Avenue. A builder called Oliver Cromwell built the church and several houses here. His grave can be found at St. Andrew's graveyard. Turn left into Cromwell Avenue and see St. Hugh's school on the right, named after Lincoln's own Saint-Bishop who rebuilt Lincoln Cathedral in the 12th Century. Margaret Thatcher visited the school in the mid 1970s to open Forbes Hall, named after the school's founder. Next door and to the left of the school building is 'Raftsund', an old 'Arts and Crafts' style house, with brick buttressing and mullioned windows, now a boarding house for the school. You are now at the crossroads with Stanhope Avenue, with Alverston Avenue ahead. On the near corner to the left is the Oglee Guest House of 1906, with fine stained glass windows and polychrome-tiled

Raftshund

floors, the name spelling out 'Our God Loves Everyone Everywhere' because its original owners had been Methodists. Opposite, across on Stanhope Avenue, is a house which became 'Dominies', the Latin name reminding us that the headmaster, Mr Forbes, the founder of St. Hugh's School, lived there in his retirement in the late 1950s. It was formerly 'Austral House'. To the right and across Alverston Avenue is 'Fairmead', now Fairmead Court, a fine house of 1986 with Gothic portals, used by the old Girls' High School and then by the boys of St. Hugh's. It had a boating pool.

Going across Stanhope Avenue and up Alverston Avenue, notice a house called 'Low Wood' on the right, at the junction with Sylvan Avenue. This house was once the home of John and Peggy Flury, after they had sold the Petwood Hotel to restaurateur Harry Plumb in 1961.

Turn left onto Sylvan Avenue and left again onto Iddesleigh Road. Most of the roads around here are named after the titles conferred upon the

Oglee Guest House

Dominies

various members of parliament who formed the original Spa syndicate in the 1880s, but one, Tarleton Avenue further up the Broadway, was named after an Irish lady who rejoiced in the effectiveness of her Spa treatments! On the Iddesleigh Road, you will see houses with turrets and unusual carved wood finials, the name of one – Bunsen House – reminding us of the many German inhabitants of the village before the first World War. Retracing your step to the junction of Iddesleigh Road with Sylvan Avenue, note the elegant Spa Court apartments which

Bunsen House

Longwood House, its verandah apparently built in the same style as that on Napoleon's house of exile on St Helena, also called 'Longwood' (corner of Iddesleigh Road & The Broadway)

replaced the much loved Spa Hotel, which had originally been the Goring Hotel, run by another German gentleman. The church of St. Peter's with its little carillon tower is next seen at the junction of Iddesleigh Road with the Broadway. You will see the Golf Hotel in all its restored splendour opposite, with its Aqua Santé Spa house further up the road. Iddesleigh Road continues across the crossroads, with the Cottage Museum on the right, and if you now cross over the Broadway you can walk towards the row of shops, some with recently restored glazed canopies and baroque style parapets. Standing with your back to the former Methodist church (now Fordman Systems) you will see, across the Broadway and to the right, a row of magnificent houses mostly designed by R.A. Came, and described in the 'Woodhall Today' section of the guide. In recent years more houses have been built on land between them, but to the same high standard and in Came's unusual vernacular. Between some gardens run narrow 'servant's paths' – another reminder of gracious Edwardian living! Walk past the first shops, and at the paved courtyard, you cannot miss the old petrol pumps with hoses on long brackets which once extended beyond the wide pavement to your car!

The Shops and the Railway

Proceed down the Broadway's mall of shops until you see a wedge shaped shop unit terminating the row. Walk on for a few feet and glance back, for at this point the old railway came into Woodhall Spa Station, one of the platforms with a bookstall (and even lending library!) being situated at the rear of the Broadway shops. Now look diagonally across from this point to the Post Office and Co-Op store, on the other side of the Broadway. The line of Clarence Road was the path of the railway line, and a big diagonal crossing brought the line to where you are now standing. Proceeding beyond the Police Station you will see on your right a small garden with a section of railway line on its sleepers, indicating the former direction and position of the rails. Moving on past the car park on your right, you see the Conservative Club on Spa Road, and further along towards the woods, the Public Conveniences, recently restored. Cross over Spa Road onto Station Road and its row of shops with Woodhall Spa's library, noticing an old painted advertisement on one gable end for 'Kathleen Poucher's…Refreshments and Catering'. Opposite these shops you will see the Mall Tavern, almost the only remaining piece of R.A. Came's great Shopping Mall, apart from the prettily half-timbered shops leading up to the little Clock Tower, to the left of the Tavern.

Finally, you arrive back at Royal Square, where the walk began.

Station Road, with the Mall Tavern and only remaining shops designed by R.A. Came

The new canopy, reinstated on the Broadway's famous row of shops

Walk 2

The Viking Way, The Hotchkin Golf Course,
Local Farms and The Bracken Golf Course

(Allow two hours for a stroll – can be muddy on large sections of the route)

Beginning outside the Cottage Museum on Iddesleigh Road, proceed Northwards across the path of the former railway, and through the white gated gravel lane. Rose Cottage, at the corner of this lane, was at various times a

The White Gate looking towards Rose Cottage

The Cottage Museum

cottage hospital and the home of entrepreneur John Lewis, who rescued the Spa Baths in the early 30s but became deeply unpopular for closing off several routes through the woods. Lewis and Sir Archibald Weigall, of Petwood House nearby, were sworn enemies.

Once through the white gate beyond the front gate of Rose Cottage, you can see:

(a) to your left, Spa Road, the Gardens of which were once Blyton's Nursery, with Coronation Hall opposite, opened in 1954 by the Earl of Ancaster for the Woodhall Spa Community.

Spa Trail

(b) Dense woodland, which, with the Hall and tennis courts, was once the site of the magnificent Victoria Hotel.
(c) Coronation Road as it goes down to the old Spa Baths, with large new houses and a restaurant which was once the Tea House in the Woods
(d) To your right, Manor Road, which we will now take.

Proceeding up the lovely tree-lined Manor Road, you will see on the right

The Dower House Hotel (17)

Originally built in 1905 for the widowed Mrs Hotchkin when her son, S.V. Hotchkin, moved in to the Manor House with his bride. The architects were Watkins & Scorer of Lincoln. On the left, you see the Bracken Golf course, and as you approach its entrance, glance back to your left over the fairways and Coalpit Wood and note one of the old Bath Houses, half-hidden by trees.

In the field which is now occupied by the first fairways and greens, the great Pageant of Lincolnshire History was held in July 1911, one of the hottest summers on record, to celebrate the finding of the Spa's waters when the first mineshaft flooded. The date is debatable. Perhaps the 1911 date for the very first minings was taken from Conway Walter's 'Records of Woodhall Spa'. Imagine local aristocrats jousting on horseback, Lady Weigall as Torfrida and Sir Archibald as a cross-gartered Hereward the Wake, and a cast of hundreds. The photographic souvenir can be seen in the Cottage Museum if specially requested.

Next to the entrance of the Bracken course is the driveway to the old Manor House where the Hotchkins lived. Today, it has a commercial

'Hereward the Wake welcomed home' in the Pageant of 1911

and residential use. The core of the building is 18th century, and the large walled garden must once have been charming. Proceeding onwards, past the driveway into the main Golf course buildings on the right, you pass the entrance to the driving range on the left, then enter a field which supplies the turf for the golf courses. It can be very muddy from now on. No cycling is allowed, and dogs must be on leads. You now walk through one of Britain's most beautiful golf courses, the Hotchkin course, across several fairways (pause and check for play in progress as each sign warns). To the far right uphill amongst the trees you can glimpse the Tower on The Moor. Eventually you emerge after a small woodland of birches onto Sandy Lane. The Viking Way* goes to the right and reconnects with the former old railway line, taking adventurous walkers to Horncastle, but our route now goes to the left down Sandy Lane, Highall Farm being the first of several farms we encounter on the right. High Hall was a medieval moated hall, likewise Whitehall, after which the nearby woods are named. Fields on the left are currently worked by Crowder's of Horncastle, who grow many trees here. A line of oak trees on the left stand opposite Chapel Farm, then a few yards beyond on the right, a red brick chapel of 1901, Wesleyan and now used by shooting parties (!) offers its handsome stone mullioned gothic window to the lane. A sequence of houses now begins on the right, in the area known

as Reeds Beck, the first three on the site of an old smithy. As you near the end of the lane, dense woodland on the left conceals several ponds made from former pits, then you reach the staggered crossroads with Reeds Beck Farm opposite on the right, and you take the left turn onto Monument Road, so called locally because you shortly come to the Wellington Monument in a field on your right. The bust of the Duke of Wellington, on top of an obelisk, is said to be facing Waterloo**, the occasion of his great victory over Napoleon in 1815. Colonel Richard Elmhirst of West Ashby erected this 36 foot high monument in 1844 in front of Waterloo Wood, which had been planted from acorns immediately after the battle.

The Wellington Monument

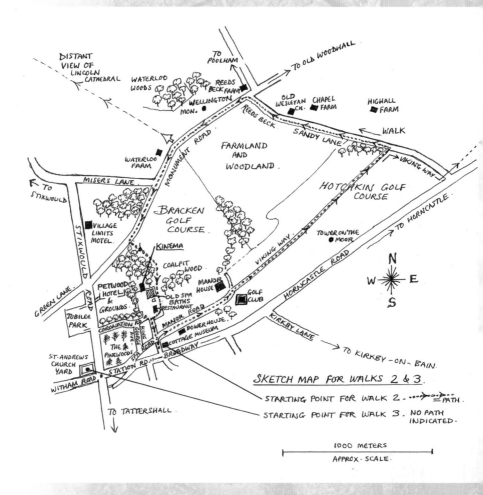

DISTANT VIEW OF LINCOLN CATHEDRAL

TO POOLHAM

TO OLD WOODHALL

WATERLOO WOODS

REEDS BECK FARM

WELLINGTON MON.

OLD WESLEYAN CHAPEL CH. FARM

HIGHALL FARM

WALK

REEDS BECK

SANDY LANE

WATERLOO FARM

MONUMENT ROAD

FARMLAND AND WOODLAND.

VIKING WAY

MISERS LANE

TO STIXWOULD

STIXWOULD ROAD

VILLAGE LIMITS MOTEL.

BRACKEN GOLF COURSE.

HOTCHKIN GOLF COURSE

TO HORNCASTLE

KINEMA

COALPIT WOOD

VIKING WAY

TOWER ON THE MOOR

PETWOOD HOTEL & GROUNDS

MANOR HOUSE

OLD SPA BATHS RESTAURANT

GOLF CLUB

HORNCASTLE ROAD

GREEN LANE.

JUBILEE PARK

CORONATION RD.

KING GEORGE AVE

MANOR ROAD

POWER HOUSE

COTTAGE MUSEUM

KIRKBY LANE

TO KIRKBY-ON-BAIN.

THE PINEWOODS

SPA RD.

BROADWAY

ST. ANDREWS CHURCH YARD

STATION RD.

WITHAM ROAD

N
W E
S

SKETCH MAP FOR WALKS 2 & 3.

TO TATTERSHALL.

STARTING POINT FOR WALK 2. —•••➤ ———➤ = PATH

STARTING POINT FOR WALK 3. NO PATH INDICATED.

1000 METERS
APPROX. SCALE.

You are now at the highest point of a small hill, and you now descend towards Waterloo Farm on the right, noting, on a clear day, between two distant stands of trees on the far right, Lincoln Cathedral on its hill. You can see it with the naked eye. On the left, Bracken Wood Cottage is a sensitively designed reminder of a picturesque old farmhouse which was derelict for many years. Next, on the right, is 'Miser's Lane' leading to a caravan park and joining the road between Stixwould and Woodhall.

The Spa Baths today, covered with Wisteria

Monument Road continues past the new Bracken Course and its lakes on the left, then you will see on the left an entrance to a public footpath bordering the woods on the Petwood Estate and the Bracken Course. Take this pathway for the fine views, and glimpses, on the right, of the Kinema in the Woods and the old Spa Baths, and emerge behind the restaurant which was once the Tea House in the Woods. Once at the front of the restaurant, turn left onto Coronation Road and as you walk towards the white gated lane at the corner, you can gauge the extent of the old Victoria Hotel, which occupied the entire length of the right hand side of the road. Walking once again through the gated lane and straight ahead, you have returned to the Cottage Museum.

* The Viking Way is described after Walk 3
** A comparison of the direction faced by the Iron Duke with any good map, and a map of Belgium showing England, will reveal that he does not face Waterloo. Nor does he face Elmhirst's West Ashby, as some have suggested.

Walk 3
Pinewoods, Parks and Gardens

(Including family activities. Allow 2 ½ hours, to include refreshments)

From the Woodhall Spa crossroad (north side) by the village War Memorial, you can walk into the graveyard and site of the former church of Langton St. Andrew, a pleasant spot where some Hotchkin family graves can be found, and, more centrally, the touching memorial sundial and seat to the Came family. The sad history of the family of Woodhall Spa's main architect can be deduced from the inscriptions on the sides of the sundial.

St Andrew's Church, graveyard and the village War Memorial

The Came family memorial

Crossing over the Stixwould Road, enter the so-called Pine Woods, looked after by the Woodland Trust. These woods were once a managed extension to the Victoria Hotel's gardens. So many paths interweave in these small woods that we will not prescribe a route, but notice the mixture of trees, and the comparative sparseness of Pine trees today. Recently the trust has introduced wooden seats and carved posts set at intervals along the paths. Can you find the 'Green Man' with his head of leaves, the Lancaster Bomber, the Woodpecker, the Pine cones and the Butterflies? There are others… which animals do they represent?

A pathway through the pinewoods

A 'Green Man' and a Lancaster carved on posts two of several provided by the Woodland Trust

Wandering eastwards you will encounter King George Avenue (named after King George V) and you will see the beautiful green and huts of the Town Bowls Club. Woodhall Spa is town-sized, but is in fact a 'Main Village'! Once on the Avenue (or you may emerge on Coronation Road which joins with it) you will see very old listed signs to the 'Rheumatism Clinic', The Kinema and the tea House in the Woods. Sadly, the clinic

(the former Spa Baths) and the Tea House are no more. But follow those signs, and emerge in the square in front of the now derelict Spa Baths, and the famous Kinema in the Woods. On a triangle of grassland you will see two huge Sequoia Wellingtonia – Sequoia Gigantea trees, which are rare in this country and much more common in Canada. Walking towards the Kinema, note on the left a dense woodland, in which you can make out an avenue of trees. These once flanked the first Spa Pleasure Grounds, which the Weigalls took on in the 1920s, and converted into an Italian garden with a central pool where the octagonal bandstand had once been. It is hard to imagine that all this area was once broad lawns, paths and flower beds.

Retrace your steps to Coronation Road by turning right once your back is to the Kinema. Walking past the pinewoods on your left, you will glimpse the Stixwould road ahead, with its beautiful bungalows, and if you cross over Stixwould Road to the pavements you can proceed to the right, and eventually see the entrance to Jubilee Park and the Cricket Ground. Further along, Maple Avenue leads to the Children's playground and a caravan park. (See entry on Jubilee Park)

Cross over Maple Avenue and prepare to cross Stixwould Road, where, on the right, is the driveway to the Petwood Hotel and grounds. (See entry on the Petwood Hotel). If you decide to explore the grounds, you will need 30 – 45 minutes. Don't miss the Petwood's own woodland of pines and silver birches, and at the southern end of the perimeter pathway round these woods, you may be able to spot an avenue of trees, beyond the ditch and through the wire-fence, which once led to the pool at the centre of the Italian Gardens. You may, in winter, be able to detect the back of the Kinema to the left of the avenue of trees, and to the East you will also glimpse the Bracken Golf Course.

The Pump Room at the Spa Baths in its heyday

Emerging from the Petwood onto Stixwould Road, you will see the lodge and former stone entrance pillars to Petwood House on the right, and, across from the lodge, at the further corner of Green Lane, a house with white painted wooden outbuildings. The Weigalls had these built as a clinic when the Spa Baths were out of action in the 1920s, and lived in the house after 1937 whenever they re-visited Woodhall from London, because the Petwood Hotel's prices had become too expensive for them! The substantial redbrick and half-timbered houses on Stixwould Road were all built by the Weigalls for their staff.

Cross over Stixwould Road onto the pavement and retrace your steps to Woodhall Spa crossroads.

Petwood Lodge which was the old gatehouse for the hotel

The Viking Way at Woodhall Spa (refer to Walk 2)

One of England's major long-distance walks, the entire Viking Way is 147 miles long and winds through many landscapes from the banks of the Humber estuary to the county of Rutland. It opened in 1976 as a result of cooperation between the Rambler's Association and the County Councils of Lincolnshire, Leicestershire and Humberside.

The Viking Way approaches Woodhall Spa from Horncastle along the former railway. Recently a team of experts have been examining ways in which the route could be improved because at present it leaves the railway path at Sandy Lane and walkers must go to the right for several hundred yards before turning left into the Hotchkin Golf Course. The former Railway route crosses by the top of the course, offering superb views of the fairways, greens and woods, but at present it is out of bounds to the public. The Way emerges from the Golf Course, continues down Manor Road, then turns left onto Iddesleigh Road, then right down Woodhall Spa's Broadway and Station Road, then across the crossroads, onto Witham Road, turning right up the new Viking Park Estate and continuing across fields to Stixwould. The Viking Way official guide book and fact sheet are available from Lincolnshire County Council outlets and from the information centres in Horncastle and at the Cottage Museum in Woodhall Spa.

Information & Services

A comprehensive list of local services can be found at
www.woodhallspa.org

In an emergency, for Fire, Police or Ambulance: **Dial 999**
The nearest hospitals with an Accident and
Emergency Department are:
Boston Pilgrim Hospital
Sibsey Road, Boston PE21 9QS Tel: 01205 364801
Lincoln County Hospital
Greetwell Road, Lincoln LN2 4AX Tel: 01522 512512

Alternatively, for medical advice, phone NHS Direct on **0845 4647**

Woodhall Spa has a First Responder service, who are community volunteers trained and equipped to deal with emergency situations, and can provide basic life support and defibrillation, after being called out by Ambulance Control.

The Neighbourhood Policing Team is based at:
Horncastle Police Station, The Wong, Horncastle, LN9 6EB
For all non-emergency calls or if you need to report an incident ring the local police station on: **01507 523332**
The Woodhall Spa Police Station is manned by local volunteers during the following hours:
Tuesday 4 – 6pm, Thursday 9.30 – 11am and Friday 2.30 – 4pm (not always on bank holidays etc) Tel: 01526 352799

Doctors Surgeries:
Dr. Butter, Tasburgh Lodge Surgery, Victoria Avenue. 01526 352466
The New Surgery, The Broadway. 01526 353888

Dentists:
The Dental Surgery, The Broadway, Woodhall Spa LN10 6SQ, Tel: 01526 352929
The Dental Studio, Victoria Lodge, The Broadway. 01526 351352

Optician;
David Hallgate, 11 Station Road, Woodhall Spa LN10 6QL
Tel: 01526 352236

Pharmacy:
Moss Chemists, The Broadway, Woodhall Spa LN10 6ST
Tel: 01526 352105

Post Office:
Woodhall Spa, 2 Clarence Road Tel: 01526 352211
Martin Dales (sub-post office), 173 Witham Road Tel: 01526 352200

Cash Machine:
HSBC Bank, The Broadway. Cashback is also available in many shops.

Travel:
The nearest train station is located at Metheringham, which links to the main Peterborough – Lincoln – Doncaster line

Buses run from Woodhall Spa to Horncastle, Boston and Lincoln
Mooring is available at Kirkstead Bridge approximately 1 mile from Woodhall Spa.

Local Towns:
Horncastle – 7 miles – market town famous for its antique shops
Boston – 18 miles – large town with many facilities. Famous for being the home of the 'Pilgrim Fathers'
Lincoln - 20 miles – City with many famous landmarks including Lincoln Castle and Cathedral. Famous for its German Style Christmas Market.

Suggestions for further Reading

**The Rev.
John Conway Walter:**   Records of Woodhall Spa and District 1904

David Robinson OBE: The book of Horncastle and Woodhall Spa

Marjorie Sargeant: A century of Golf at Woodhall Spa
Voices of Woodhall Spa – A Century of
Memories
Woodhall Spa and the World 1885 – 1890
Echoes of Woodhall Spa (The Spa
in Wartime)

Edward Mayor: Petwood – the remarkable Story of a
Famous Lincolnshire Hotel
The Kinema in The Woods – The story of
Woodhall Spa's Unique Cinema

Brian & Shirley Prince: Woodhall Spa on Old Picture Postcards
– Yesterday's Lincolnshire Series No. 1

Richard Latham: The Definitive Guide to the Hotchkin
Course, Woodhall Spa

Twinning Association

Contact Jack Baker 01526 352997

Woodhall Spa is twinned with the French village of Röèze sur Sarthe near Le Mans. The Twinning charter was signed there in October 1988 and then in Woodhall in the spring of 1989. French families visit Woodhall for 4 or 5 days in the spring and host families are always needed. Similarly, Woodhall's teenagers and families visit Roeze using flights from Stansted to Tours. Many visits have been made both ways since 1988, and long-lasting friendships have been forged. Recently the Twinning Association formed its own caravanning group and it is hoped that rallies will be arranged in the near future. Situated on the banks of the River Sarthe, Roeze is a small village with a few shops but only one pub and restaurant. The friendly people love coming over to Woodhall, and everyone in the Association enjoys the contrasting cultures, specially arranged coach outings and meals.

England's Unique Cinema

THE KINEMA IN THE WOODS

Coronation Road, Woodhall Spa

Situated in the beautiful woodlands of this delightful Spa town, this unique cinema uses rear projection to show the latest films nightly, with matinées at weekends and during the school holidays.
Large car park. Full disabled access.

Home to the famous Compton Organ, played every Saturday during the intermission of the main film.
Also a feature of our "Down Memory Lane" nostalgia shows which take place regularly on weekday afternoons from March to December.
Phone for more details.

24 hour information line
01526 352166
www.thekinemainthewoods.co.uk

R. J. Hirst

HIGH CLASS FAMILY BUTCHERS

OF WOODHALL SPA.

Russell Hirst has earned an excellent reputation as a Butcher for over 20 years, he has recently been nominated as UKTV Food Hero and voted Horncastle News Super Server Runner Up. He specialises in delicious Hand made Lincolnshire sausages and haslets, made daily from best quality local pork and contains no colourings, additives or artificial preservatives.

An excellent selection of high quality meat sourced from local farmers with complete traceability is available Tuesday to Saturday from their chilled displays.

Lincolnshire Sausage Rolls, Haslets and Dry Roasted Ham are oven baked daily in the shop. Delicious range of Curtis products, award winning preserves and Myers Famous Plum Loaf.

Open: Tue, Thur, Fri 8am – 5pm
Wed 8am – 1pm, Sat 8am – 3pm

Come and visit the shop (next door to The Mall)
Station Rd, Woodhall Spa. Tel 01526 352321

LOCALLY SOURCED PRODUCE

Tastes of Lincolnshire

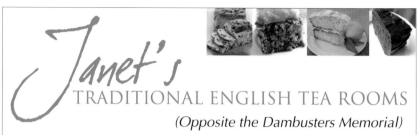

Janet's
TRADITIONAL ENGLISH TEA ROOMS
(Opposite the Dambusters Memorial)
A range of home-made cakes and light lunches

Dambusters and other RAF Memorabilia
Local produce & Bric-a-Brac

Open 7 Days a Week
7.30am - 5.00pm

18 Station Road, Woodhall Spa
Lincolnshire LN10 6QL
Proprietor Janet Hunt

CLAREMONT
GUEST HOUSE
9/11 Witham Road
WOODHALL SPA

B&B FROM £20 - Single • Double • Twin • Family
Ensuite Rooms • Off Street Parking

Within easy reach of Lincoln, Boston, the coast and the Wolds
WOODHALL SPA makes an excellent centre for exploring the
county, or for relaxing and enjoying a variety of unusual attractions
for all the family. The peaceful, charming, wooded environment
provides a veritable oasis for the traveller and the CLAREMONT
offers a homely B&B in a traditional, unspoilt Victorian guest
house. Excellent choice of food within walking distance.

TELEPHONE 01526 35-20-00

HOTEL · RESTAURANT
BANQUETING
WEDDINGS
CONFERENCE CENTRE

The Petwood Hotel is a an attractive building set in 30 acres of mature woodland with rhododendron walks, extensive lawns, gardens and a lake.

Inside the hotel has many original features including extensive oak panelling and a magnificent main staircase. There are 53 en-suit bedrooms decorated to a high standard.

The hotel has unrivalled function and banqueting facilities. The Garden Room is perfect for smaller parties, whilst the elegant Petwood Suite is ideally suited to larger gatherings where upto 120 guests can be accommodated, The Woodland Suite can accommodate up to 200 guests.

The Tennysons restaurant specialises in local produce whilst light lunches and afternoon teas are served daily on the terrace and in the bar overlooking the magnificent gardens.

For further information visit the website on www.petwood.co.uk or telephone 01526 352411

Stixwould Rd, Woodhall Spa, Lincs LN10 6QG
Telephone 01526 352411 · Fax 01526 353473
email reception@petwood.co.uk
www.petwood.co.uk

ABBEY LODGE INN

Tattershall Rd, Kirkstead, Woodhall Spa, Lincolnshire LN10 6UQ

Open for Lunch and Evening Meals Monday to Saturday
Closed All Day Sunday
Traditional Family Run Pub with Function Suite

Telephone 01526 352538

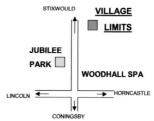

Mill House circa 1906? Photo courtesy of Derek Holmes

There has been a warm, welcoming home in Kirkstead, down by the river Witham for more than 150 years, but now the invitation is extended to all who would appreciate the tranquil setting of KIRKSTEAD OLD MILL COTTAGE as Barbara and Tony Hodgkinson, who have cared for the house for 35 of those years, are delighted to be offering bed and breakfast, in three double or twin en suite guest rooms, to those who want to "get away from it all".

Or perhaps you want a friendly, comfortable place to stay in while you play golf, visit the local Battle of Britain Flight Museum or relatives in Woodhall Spa. The Kingfisher Suite, on the ground floor, has been purpose built to meet the needs of those with limited mobility or other disabilities. You will be welcome to come and go as you please, and there are two guest lounges, a ¾ acre garden and abundant wild life along the riverbank and in our 6-acre wild garden for you to enjoy. To find out more about us, please ring 01526 35 36 37 or look at our detailed Web site: www.woodhallspa.com

Welcome
to Excellence

LOCALLY
SOURCED
PRODUCE

Tastes of Lincolnshire

Kirkstead Old Mill Cottage Photo by Neil Storey 2006

98

The Hotchkin Course
No.1 inland course in the UK
GOLF MAGAZINE **No. 53 in the world**

WOODHALL SPA
THE NATIONAL GOLF CENTRE

The Hotchkin Course
Recently voted the best inland course in the UK by Golf World, the Hotchkin Course sits amidst wonderful natural surroundings and offers an exquisite and memorable golfing experience.

The Bracken Course
The Donald Steel designed Bracken Course, opened in 1998, complements the Hotchkin perfectly with its large, undulating greens and numerous water hazards.

Practice Facilities
The National Golf Centre has extensive practice facilities, including one of Europe's finest short game academies and a 20 bay (floodlit) driving range.

Conference & Catering
Visitors may also take advantage of the conference and catering facilities as part of their golf day. Up to 180 guests can be accommodated at any one time.

The Golf Shop
The golf shop stocks a superb range of merchandise, including National Golf Centre branded items, as well as clothing and equipment from all the top golfing brands.

WOODHALL SPA - THE HOME OF ENGLISH GOLF

The Broadway, Woodhall Spa, Lincs LN10 6PU
T: 01526 352511 · F: 01526 351817 · E: booking@englishgolf union.org · W: www.woodhallspagolf.com

⑤ SILK ORCHID
ORIENTAL RESTAURANT

FINE CUISINE FROM THAILAND, CHINA & MALAYSIA

OPENING TIMES
Open 7 Days
Lunchtime
12.00 noon to 2.00pm
Evening
5.30pm to 11.00pm

PARTY EVENTS WELCOME
with advanced booking

Station Road
Woodhall Spa
LN10 6QL
T: 01526 353567
www.silkorchidrestaurant.co.uk

About the author

Edward Mayor was born in Sheffield in 1947 and has lived in Lincoln for fourteen years, St Ives in Cornwall for four years, and now lives at Reeds Beck near Woodhall Spa. A life Friend of Lincoln cathedral, he is an art historian, recitalist, artist and author of four other books about Lincolnshire, its artists and Woodhall Spa. This year saw the publication of his first compact disc: 'From Sheffield to Lincolnshire – Edward Mayor Reads'. For decades a scholar of all things oriental, he performs the Japanese Tea Ceremony in a Tea House and Garden of his own design, and travels widely in Holland. He and his partner Jonathan Perks share a love of 20th Century Classical Music and their terrier Rosie has featured on television and accompanies them wherever they go.